Color
Me
Mindful

SEASONS

Anastasia Catris

GALLERY BOOKS

NEW YORK LONDON TORONTO SYDNEY NEW DELHI

G

Gallery Books
An Imprint of Simon & Schuster, Inc.
1230 Avenue of the Americas
New York, NY 10020

Copyright © 2015 by Orion
Originally published in Great Britain in 2015 by Orion, an imprint of the Orion Publishing Group Ltd.
Published by arrangement with the Orion Publishing Group Ltd.

First Gallery Books trade paperback edition January 2017

GALLERY BOOKS and colophon are registered trademarks of Simon & Schuster, Inc.

For information about special discounts for bulk purchases, please contact Simon & Schuster Special Sales at 1-866-506-1949 or business@simonandschuster.com.

The Simon & Schuster Speakers Bureau can bring authors to your live event. For more information or to book an event, contact the Simon & Schuster Speakers Bureau at 1-866-248-3049 or visit our website at www.simonspeakers.com.

Manufactured in the United States of America

1 3 5 7 9 10 8 6 4 2

ISBN 978-1-5011-6234-3

Color Me Mindful

Books in the Color Me Mindful series:

Color Me Mindful: Birds

Color Me Mindful: Butterflies

Color Me Mindful: Enchanted Creatures

Color Me Mindful: Seasons

Color Me Mindful: Tropical

Color Me Mindful: Underwater

Introduction

Mindfulness is the art of present moment awareness, of being alert and relaxed at once. Art is a wonderful gateway to this state. As you color with focus and attention, your stress will start to fade. As you watch closely to stay within the lines, your worries will seem to lessen. And as you lose yourself in the wonders of color and creativity, your surroundings will come alive and seem a little brighter.

It's a busy world we live in and you might sometimes feel as if life is rushing by, one thing after another. For many, this rushing is code for that thing we call stress, that constant striving to find happiness through one more success, through one more experience, leading to a feeling of exhaustion and a massive to-do list!

If your world feels like this, it's time to slow down. So put down your tasks, your goals, and your worries, just for a moment (or maybe an hour). Allow yourself to recharge by taking a little holiday from thinking, stepping into the present moment, and coloring in the beautiful shapes and patterns in this book.

Take a breath and feel the air coming and going. Pick up a crayon and begin to gradually fill this world with color. Let this moment be as it is. Learning to focus and enjoy simple things like coloring once more can lead to the happiness everyone deserves.

Oli Doyle

Author of *Mindfulness Plain & Simple* and *Mindfulness for Life*

www.peacethroughmindfulness.com.au

About the Author

After graduating from Royal Holloway, University of London with a BA Honors in English Literature, Anastasia Catris traveled to the United States to pursue her passion for illustration by studying at The Kubert School of Cartoon and Graphic Art.

She returned to the UK in 2009, and has since worked as a freelance illustrator for HarperCollins, *Kerrang!*, Fox, Marvel, DC, and *Cygnus Alpha: The Doctor Who Fanzine*. Ana lives in Wales, United Kingdom, and is an advocate of art therapy and of the calming power of coloring in.

www.anastasiacatris.com
Instagram: @AnastasiaCatris